About the Author

Ryan Cochrane is a graduate of the University of Massachusetts where he has earned degrees in History and Sociology. His interests include reading, nature, history, ideas, science fiction and spending time with his dog, Scrappy Junior.

Nana Scrappy

Ryan Cochrane

Nana Scrappy

Olympia Publishers

London

www.olympiapublishers.com
OLYMPIA PAPERBACK EDITION

A CIP catalogue record for this title is
available from the British Library.

ISBN: 978-1-78830-056-8

First Published in 2018
Olympia Publishers
60 Cannon Street
London
EC4N 6NP

Dedication

I would like to dedicate this book to my parents, Walter and Marie Cochrane. They always inspired and encouraged my imagination. I would also like to dedicate this to my beloved Yorkshire Terrier, Scrappy – a loyal, gentle, and courageous little friend. He was my constant companion from 2005 to 2016.

Acknowledgments

So many people helped and encouraged me in writing my first book that I beg their forgiveness if I fail to acknowledge them here. This couldn't have been done without the inspiration and encouragement of my parents and family, especially my grandparents. I grew up seeing my grandparents on a weekly basis and was regaled with stories from another age. My first-grade teacher Miss White introduced me to the classics of children's literature during daily story time, and my fifth-grade teacher Mr. Shawn Gough helped me run my Save the Greyhounds Campaign that provided food, water, blankets and other supplies to greyhound dogs who were too old to race anymore and needed homes. My incredible illustrator Jessica McCarthy of Portland, Maine, Steve Law of Thinking Man Films, and the input of my professors Dr. Tom Turner and Dr. Mike Behe whose help was indispensable in getting this story published — much thanks to all of you!

Many years ago, in a house near a gently rolling river, there lived Nana Scrappy and her loyal gardener, Eugene O'Squirrel. It was with them that I learned the value of selflessness and forgiveness.

Nana Scrappy's house was large and white, with a funny polka dot fence that reminded people of a cow's spots. Beside the well in the garden was a little bitty house where Eugene O'Squirrel lived with his wife Ethel, and his sons Ephraim and Edward. You could see them all in the garden on sunny days: Nana Scrappy in her favorite pink muumuu embroidered with yellow flowers, and Eugene the squirrel in his tweed flat cap and trusty old gardening jacket mended repeatedly over the years. His corduroy trousers had a big round hole in the back for his furry tail.

Nana Scrappy was so happy Eugene was her gardener. He was a dear friend as well as a loyal employee. In his youth, Eugene had been a scout in the British Army. After all, who is better than a squirrel at climbing trees and seeing for great distances? But those adventures were in the past. Nowadays, there was nothing Eugene enjoyed more than getting a fire going and using the many good things that grew in Nana Scrappy's garden to make his favorite stew. Many a time, the local forest animals dropped by to sample Eugene's cooking and his world famous homemade acorn ale – a beverage Nana Scrappy frowned upon, though she couldn't resist paying him a visit whenever she caught a whiff of the delicious stew simmering in his tiny fireplace.

Nana Scrappy loved her friends and family, but she had her habits, and was most particular about sticking to them. She always had breakfast, lunch and dinner at the same hour of each day of each year. In her house, she had to have things *her* way, but this was sometimes difficult because of Eugene's mischievous nature. There was, you see, a dumbwaiter elevator for taking food from the downstairs pantry up to the other floors of Nana Scrappy's house. Nana Scrappy, the O'Squirrels and other furry guests were small enough to ride in it along with the food trundling up from the pantry. Eugene was the elevator operator and sometimes he liked to pull the lever too fast. Once, Nana Scrappy was bringing some flour up to the kitchen from the pantry and Eugene pulled the lever so sharply, the elevator ride resembled a rollercoaster! When Eugene finally stopped laughing, Nana Scrappy was covered in flour and vowed never to ride in the elevator again. She was so upset she almost fired him.

Eugene wouldn't be the first gardener Nana Scrappy had fired. A great big guinea pig named Sparfield worked for Nana Scrappy while Eugene was in the army. Sparfield was a jolly fellow said all the forest animals, but he had done something so naughty - even naughtier than anything Eugene could come up with - that Nana Scrappy had banished him from her estate forever. Eugene didn't fancy going the same way as Sparfield, so he made Nana Scrappy some of his stew as an apology, and they were soon the best of friends once more.

Life was good, Nana Scrappy was thinking to herself as she poured another cup of herbal tea. The doorbell rang. Who could this be? she wondered as she opened the door. There before her appeared the short and hairy figure of her grandson, Barry. The little puppy was clad in his best khaki shorts, green jacket and a red bow tie. His glistening white doggie shoes were covered in mud. "Hi, Nana Scrappy!" Barry ruffed as he ran around in circles.

"Now, a proper dog doesn't chase his own tail. If your grandfather were here…"

"Aw, come on, Nana Scrappy. I'm just happy to see you! I'm staying with you for my summer vacation."

"Oh, how nice," Nana Scrappy said, gazing through her spectacles at her grandson and his waggly tail. She imagined all the fun they'd have together. Baking, playing board games, reading stories… Nana Scrappy was so caught up dreaming about all these lovely things, she almost didn't hear what Barry had said. "All summer?" she gasped.

"Don't you remember, Nana Scrappy? My dad is going on a long business trip and he thought this would be the perfect opportunity for me to spend some quality time with you!"

"Well, I suppose you'd better come in," Nana Scrappy sighed. She *had* forgotten. Tonight was the night she was meant to host a dinner for her Ladies Society friends. A very important dinner, in fact. Nana Scrappy was going to be presented with an award for her superb homegrown cabbages. She had gotten so wrapped up in planning the perfect evening, she had quite forgotten she had promised to look after her very active and very messy grandson. The unexpected arrival of Barry disrupted her schedule. And as much as she loved the little puppy, if there was anything that got Nana Scrappy worked up, it was when her plans were spoiled.

Barry wasted no time and bolted into the house, his muddy doggie shoes tracking filth everywhere, and

started sniffing around.

"Barry! Your shoes are all muddy. Get back here and wipe them off on the doormat! I'm hosting a very important dinner tonight. I'm to receive a prize for my cabbages, but look at this mess..."

"Wow, Nana Scrappy. Your house smells so different from my house." Barry stopped sniffing and stood as still as a statue. "I'm hungry. Do I smell burgies?"

Nana Scrappy grimaced. "Burgies? Is that what your father feeds you all the time? Hamburgers? A puppy should be eating his puppy food so he can grow big and–"

Before Nana Scrappy could finish, Barry bolted into the kitchen, sniffing around excitedly. There was Eugene, cooking hamburgers and flipping them over with his tail.

"Are those what I think they are?" asked Barry.

Eugene O'Squirrel smiled down at the hungry puppy. "They sure are. Have a seat, Barry, my boy, they'll be ready in a jiffy!"

Barry jumped up on the chair at Nana Scrappy's kitchen table, all laid out with her best silverware ready for her important guests. Eugene brought a heaped plate of freshly cooked hamburgers over. Eugene grinned, as squirrels often do, as he put a hot and juicy burgie onto Barry's dinner plate.

Just as Barry was about to bite down on his favorite treat, Nana Scrappy burst through the kitchen door. "Wait a second! I have Barry's dinner right here."

Barry's smile melted away. Between Nana Scrappy's paws was a bag of healthy, dry dog food designed by scientists especially for puppies.

"But Eugene cooked me burgers!" Barry protested.

Nana Scrappy scowled and dumped the dog food that resembled a mound of dirt onto Barry's plate.

"You are lucky you get to eat your dinner on a nice, clean plate; most puppies your age eat out of a dog dish," Nana Scrappy said. "Mind you don't make a mess. This table has to be just how I like it when my guests arrive."

Barry went over to his dish and sniffed, then jumped back in disgust. Does Nana Scrappy hate me? Barry thought to himself. Doesn't she want me to spend school vacation with her?

Nana Scrappy wagged her paw at Barry. "Now, Barry, eat up, and you'll grow up big and strong."

Barry sidled toward the smelly mess of dog food before him. Surely it couldn't taste as bad as it looked. After all, it looked like dirt. And it smelled like dirt. But

Barry was a good little dog, so he took a small bite... AND IT TASTED LIKE DIRT, TOO!

"Nana Scrappy, I can't eat this and I won't eat this!"

"Barry James Furryman, you will sit here until you clean your plate. I am hosting a dinner party tonight and I don't want any trouble!"

Barry was having none of this. He jumped down off his chair and ran out of the kitchen.

"Barry, come back!" Nana Scrappy cried. But it was too late. Her grandson was gone. "Eugene, we must look for him. He'll tramp dirt all over the house and the Ladies' Society won't give me my prize. Look upstairs. I will look here on the ground floor."

Eugene rose to attention, gave Nana Scrappy a soldierly salute and sprang into action, scurrying across the kitchen floor. He had been one of the finest scouts in the British Army's Squirrel Corps. Nana Scrappy was comforted in the knowledge that no one would perform a more thorough search for Barry than Eugene.

Nana Scrappy started searching the ground floor for Barry. First stop: the library. "Barry!" she barked, sniffing in every corner of the room. "Barry! Come on back now."

Nana Scrappy noticed a little piece of paper on the desk near the reading chair in her library. It was a note from Barry!

Nana Scrappy,

It seems like you don't want me here. So I left and am
on my way back home.
I'm sorry if I made you mad.
Your loving grandson,

Barry

Nana Scrappy's eyes teared up as she read the note. On his way home? But it would be getting dark soon.

Eugene O'Squirrel entered the library. "I couldn't find Barry, Nana Scrappy," he squeaked as he jumped up onto the table where Barry's note lay. "Hmm… what's this?" Eugene pulled his reading glasses out of his tweed jacket. "Why, according to this, Barry has run away!"

"I know, I know," Nana Scrappy said. "What if he gets lost in the forest?"

"Well, we gotta find him! But we're going to need some help."

As the sun began to set, Nana Scrappy and Eugene set off to find Barry. As they hurried out into the estate where shadows were already growing in the twilight gloom, they heard a car approaching. To their relief, it was Nana Scrappy's son Harold in his beloved red convertible car with its shiny silver bumpers. Harold was a dashing dog with a heart of gold; an archeologist who traveled the world discovering lost secrets of the past. He waved his hat in greeting as he screeched to a halt.

"Harold, thank goodness you're here," Nana Scrappy yipped, giving her son a hug.

"I'm hardly going to miss my mama winning the most prestigious cabbage award I've ever heard of, am I? But what's this? You're upset."

"Little Barry's gone missing," Nana Scrappy said. "And I am going to miss my dinner party!"

"I can't believe you are thinking about your dinner party at a time like this," Harold said. "But never fear! I, of course, have a plan of action..."

And with that, Harold, Nana Scrappy and Eugene set out to survey the area for Barry.

"Barry!" They called the puppy's name to no avail. They sniffed under every bush and checked under every rock. Eugene scurried up trees and called for him across the forest. The rest of the O'Squirrel family gave the inside of the house another look, in case Barry came back to get at the leftover burgies.

"What if he is hungry or hurt or has been captured by pirates?" Nana Scrappy fretted.

Before Harold could comfort her, a twig snapped and Eugene landed right in front of them.

"Anything to report?" Harold asked.

"Nothing," Eugene said. "I covered the entire area by jumping from tree to tree."

Harold noticed the clear blue sky growing darker with every passing minute. The birds were chirping their evening song and a frog hopped through the grass on his way to bed. This place is perfect, thought Harold. It was a grrrrreat place to grow up! All the sounds in the forest joined in a chorus of bird song, soft breezes and babbling brooks. The fragrance of the summer air was bliss to

Harold. Everything would have been just perfect, if only little Barry had not run off.

"Oh, how could you, Barry?" Nana Scrappy put her head in her paws. "I'm going to miss my award ceremony! And I was so looking forward to it."

"What was it that set him off in the first place?" Harold asked.

"She wouldn't let him eat burgies," Eugene squeaked.

Harold's jaw dropped. "You wouldn't let him eat burgies? Why, when I was a boy, that's all you fed me."

"I know, I know. I just thought a good grandmother should feed her grandson wholesome and nutritious food," Nana Scrappy said, lying down on the grass. Her old legs were too weary to go on. "But I'm a terrible grandmother. Barry's lost and all alone."

"Eugene, why don't you continue the search while I make a fire and let Nana Scrappy rest her feet?" Harold suggested. He gathered kindling for a fire. Rubbing her sore paws, Nana Scrappy's imagination began to conjure up images of all the terrible things that might be happening to Barry.

"What if coyotes got him?" Nana Scrappy asked herself, her eyes filling with tears.

"Now, now, don't say that," Harold said. "I'm sure he will be all right."

All of a sudden, the sound of crashing trees came from the woods.

"What on earth?" Harold asked, startled.

The sound of trees being knocked over grew louder and closer.

"Eugene, is that you?" Harold called out nervously. Something big was moving closer. Something far too large to be Eugene. A bulldozer? Some kind of bear? Harold hid Nana Scrappy behind a bush. Whatever it was, if it had Barry, Harold knew he might have to fight it - alone.

The noise grew louder and louder until finally a large, furry animal thundered out of the woods and almost rolled right on top of them.

"It can't be!" Nana Scrappy emerged from the bush. She was so amazed, she struggled to get the words out. "Why it's..."

"Sparfield!" The gigantic guinea pig squeaked. "Hi, Nana Scrappy!"

Eugene was riding on Sparfield's shoulder. "Look who I found in the woods," said the wily squirrel. "To be fair, it doesn't take an army scout to find something this loud."

Nana Scrappy's doggie legs began to go wobbly. Harold caught her before she fell.

"You know this creature?" Harold asked Nana Scrappy.

"You don't remember me, Harold?" Sparfield said in his high-pitched voice. "I guess it's been years..."

"*That* Sparfield?" Harold woofed. "I haven't seen you since I was a puppy!"

Then Eugene said, "This is the fella who was the gardener before me, isn't it? The one you fired?"

Nana Scrappy, still slightly woozy, held onto Harold. "That's him. If you can call such a troublesome animal a gardener."

Sparfield grinned and let out a huge burp.

"Ewwww!" Harold and Eugene said, holding their noses as the cloud of green vapor rolled from the guinea pig's mouth.

Sparfield's cheeks turned pink and he giggled, placing his paw over his mouth. "Excuse me. I was snacking on a few trees when I smelled the smoke from your fire!" He wiped his runny nose with his paw. "I hoped there'd be toasted marshmallows."

"What could Sparfield have done that was so bad you fired him?" Eugene asked.

"Oh boy, this is gonna be good!" Sparfield said as he sat his enormous body on one of the little logs beside their roaring fire.

Nana Scrappy began her tale. "Well, Eugene, when Harold was a little pup, I needed someone to weed my flowerbeds and take care of my vegetables. Harold always wanted to be an archaeologist, and whenever he tried to help me do the weeding, he'd dig up huge holes amongst my prized cucumbers, searching for dinosaur bones."

Sparfield chuckled and spoke up, "I was much better than Harold at weeding. I was so good at it, I ate all of the weeds, all of the flowers, all the vegetables and the apple pies that were cooling on the windowsill near the garden. I even bit a piece out of the side of the house!" Sparfield grinned. "It's all true."

Nana Scrappy ruffed. "Tell Eugene about the well!"

Sparfield blushed.

"Well, I- I was fetching some water for Nana Scrappy from the well near the house. I have very bad allergies and I was covered in pollen from all the weeding. I sneezed and little Harold, who was standing on top of the well helping me... he fell into it! Thankfully he was able to catch ahold of a stone that was sticking out, otherwise he would have fallen all the way down."

Harold's eye bulged. "You didn't mention how deep and dangerous it is!"

"It took two hours for a team of workers with a new rope to get him out of there - I had no idea it was so deep," Sparfield continued.

"And dark," chimed in Harold. He shivered as he remembered the long ordeal.

"Nana Scrappy said that was the last straw. I was kicked out and I've lived in the woods ever since."

"Well, what are you doing here now?" Harold asked the giant guinea pig.

"Why, Ethel O'Squirrel and her sons ran into me after they finished searching Nana Scrappy's house for Barry. I thought I would come and see if you needed some help."

Nana Scrappy frowned. "That's very kind of you, Sparfield, but we are running out of time. I just don't know what to do. We are going to miss my award dinner! I worked so hard on those cabbages. And I laid the table just how I like it..."

Harold, Eugene and Sparfield all stood around Nana Scrappy, their expressions begging Nana Scrappy to continue the search. She thought hard. As much as she was looking forward to the Ladies Society telling her what a great job she'd made of her beloved garden, she knew in her heart there would always be more cabbages and more awards. There was only one Barry, and she loved him.

Nana Scrappy dried her tears. "Eugene?" she said. "I want you to run back to the house and cancel the dinner party."

Eugene was puzzled. Nana Scrappy had been planning this dinner for months.

"My mind is made up. Go to the house and use the telephone to call each of the guests and let them know that no dinner party is more important to me than my grandson."

Eugene sprang to attention, saluted Nana Scrappy, then swung about-face and scampered back toward Nana Scrappy's house.

Watching Eugene disappear into the distance, Nana Scrappy knew she had made the right decision. She was sore about the award ceremony, but she knew there would be no joy in receiving a prize if Barry wasn't there to enjoy it with her. As she told herself this, Nana Scrappy caught a glimpse of a red piece of cloth caught on some nearby bushes. "What is that?" Nana Scrappy asked as she tottered over to investigate. "Why, it's Barry's bow tie!"

Harold and Sparfield exchanged worried glances. "Over there, look! Off in the distance - a shoe!" Harold yelped.

The three scrambled over and found a white doggie shoe covered in mud, flung into a bunch of weeds.

"This is definitely Barry's shoe. He must have been running from something," said Nana Scrappy. Poor Barry. How could she ever have contemplated stopping the search for something as silly as a party?

"Or toward something," Sparfield squeaked as he pointed towards Nana Scrappy's house.. "Look"

The three headed to the house. As they did, Eugene scurried out of the front door to meet them. "I made the phone calls like you asked, Nana Scrappy."

"Very good, Eugene," she sighed.

"No luck finding Barry?" Eugene asked.

Nana Scrappy hung her head. She spotted some doggie footprint tracks leading from the entrance gate and towards the well. "Everybody! Look!"

"Why, these must be Barry's tracks," said Harold, pulling out his magnifying glass. "Indeed they are. And they lead to the well."

"Let us waste no time. Onward!" squeaked Sparfield.

As they ran to the well, they heard the faint sound of whimpering. "Barry! Barry!" Their cries echoed down the deep, dark well. Staring down, they saw only blackness. Nana Scrappy leaned over the edge, trying to catch a glimpse of her grandson.

"I'm in here, Nana Scrappy!" Barry barked.

"Barry! Are you all right?" Nana Scrappy yelped.

"Hurry, Nana Scrappy, it's dark and scary in here! I think there might be a ghost, too!"

To everyone's surprise, it was then that Sparfield took charge. "Grab ahold of my arms, Harold. Nana Scrappy, you grab ahold of Harold's back legs. Eugene, you grab onto Nana Scrappy's legs. That way we can make a ladder to rescue Barry!"

"OK, let's do it," Eugene commanded, and they all got in line and formed a chain, lowering themselves into the deep dark well. Eugene went first, because he was a brave squirrel with excellent eyesight. Big ol' Sparfield acted as the anchor, standing firm and holding onto his friends' legs so they wouldn't topple into the well.

"Barry, here we come. Grab hold of Eugene's tail when he reaches down to you," Nana Scrappy instructed the pup.

Barry was very frightened but he managed to utter a short yelp. "OK, Nana Scrappy!"

"Have you reached him yet?" squeaked Sparfield.

"Almost," the squirrel said as he stretched and stretched to reach Barry's tail.

"Let me know if you can grab his tail." Nana Scrappy yelped, stretching as far as her old bones would let her.

"I... I... I got him!" Eugene chirped. "I got Barry!"

Nana Scrappy let out a sigh of great relief. "OK, Sparfield! Pull us back out of this well!"

Sparfield pulled on the chain of furry creatures and drew them out of the well. Sparfield pulled so hard and so fast that the chain broke and flung everyone up into the air. Some of them landed on the grass near the well and Eugene ended up in a nearby tree.

After Nana Scrappy struggled to her feet, she gave Barry a big doggie hug.

"Barry! Never, ever do anything like that ever again!" She tried to scold him, but her tail kept wagging back and forth. Everyone could see how happy she was.

Barry's little tail wagged in time with hers. "I'm sorry, Nana Scrappy. I was sulking about the burgers, so I ran out of the house, got lost in the woods, heard a crash of thunder and got scared. I ran, lost my bow tie and my shoes."

"A crash of thunder, eh?" Harold said, looking slyly at Sparfield.

"Oh, hi, Uncle Harold!" Barry barked. "But – oh dear – Nana Scrappy. Didn't you miss your award dinner?" Barry asked.

"Barry, there are simply some things that are more important than awards," Nana Scrappy said as she embraced her grandson, his little tail wagging. "Why don't we all go back to the house? I'm sure there are whole plates with piles of uneaten burgies on them."

At that, Barry began running around in circles and jumping on and off Nana Scrappy, Harold, Sparfield and even little Eugene.

Nut
BROW

"Easy, easy boy," Harold said with a grin.

As the hungry adventurers arrived back at the house, Nana Scrappy thought she smelled something funny. As she went through the doggie door, she almost tripped flat on her face with shock.

"SURPRISE!"

An enormous crowd of animals and people appeared from behind chairs, couches, potted plants and the grandfather clock. Everyone who had been invited to the award dinner was there.

"Why, Eugene," cried Nana Scrappy. "I thought I told you to cancel the award ceremony."

The squirrel's eyes shone with laughter. "Well, Nana Scrappy, we all knew how important it was to you, so we decided to surprise you."

"Oh, but I don't deserve this. I'm a terrible, terrible dog," Nana Scrappy whimpered.

Barry walked over and put his paw on her shoulder. "Nana Scrappy, you left everything, including your award dinner, to come find me. If anything, you deserve more recognition than just a prize for your garden vegetables. You deserve a Great Grandma award."

All the guests nodded in agreement.

That night, there was an award ceremony by candlelight, and all the animals and people feasted on the most delicious burgies they ever tasted. The O'Squirrels dined on nutloaf and vegetables from the garden and Sparfield ate a chair, part of the dining room curtain, a lamp, and washed it all down with Eugene's signature acorn ale. I wag my tail just thinking about that night.

How do I know all this? Because from then on, Nana Scrappy and I were inseparable; *but this was only the beginning of our adventures.*

Barry

9 781788 300568